D0753362

DATE DUE			

62586

921
CHA

Dell, Pamela.

Michael Chang :
tennis champion

SISKIYOU COUNTY OFFICE OF
EDUCATION, LIBRARY

664366 01365   19121A   001

MICHAEL CHANG
Tennis Champion

*"There's no shortcut to success.
Hard work is the only way to go."*

MICHAEL CHANG
Tennis Champion

By Pamela Dell

CHILDRENS PRESS ®
CHICAGO

PHOTO CREDITS

AP/Wide World — title, half title, 7 (left), 31, 32
Reuters/Bettman — cover, 5, 22 (left), 26, 27, 28, 29, 30
Focus on Sports — 7 (right), 22 (right)
Courtesy Mr. and Mrs. Joe Chang — 8 (left and right), 9, 10,
  11, 12, 13 (left and right), 15, 17 (left and right), 18, 19, 21, 24
Michael Baz — 25

EDITORIAL STAFF

Project Editor: E. Russell Primm III
Design and Electronic Composition: Biner Design
Photo Research: Carol Parden

ACKNOWLEDGMENTS

The author and editors would like to thank Michael and his
family for their gracious assistance and cooperation on this
biography. The book would not have been possible without
them. Additionally, Tom Ross of Advantage International,
Michael Chang's management representative, was
unfailingly supportive and enthusiastic. His contributions
are evident throughout the book.

Library of Congress Cataloging-in-Publication Data
Dell, Pamela.
    Michael Chang : (tennis champion) / by Pamela Dell.
    p. cm. — (Picture story biography)
    Summary: A biography of the Chinese American tennis
player who, in 1989, became the youngest man to win the
prestigious French Open tournament.
    ISBN 0-516-04185-1
    1. Chang, Michael, 1972– —Juvenile literature. 2.
Tennis players — United States — Juvenile literature. [1.
Chang, Michael, 1972– . 2. Tennis players. 3. Chinese
Americans—Biography.] I. Title. II. Series: Picture-story
biographies.

GV994.C47D45 1992   92-6384
796.342'092—dc20   CIP
[B]   AC

Michael came on strong at the 1989 French Open.

THE TENNIS BALL flies wild. It hits the net and bounces out of bounds. Thousands of fans jammed together in the stadium leap to their feet in sudden chaos — the opponent has double-faulted! The young American thrusts his arms in the air, triumphant! He is barely seventeen but victory is his. Now his name will be well-known throughout the world of sports. His name is Michael Chang.

This was the scene at Roland Garros Stadium in Paris, France, in June 1989. While the world watched, young Michael Chang had beaten the world's top-ranked tennis player, Ivan Lendl. Their match had worn on for more than four painful hours. By the final moments of the game Michael's legs were so cramped he could barely walk. He was hot and thirsty and tired to the bone. But in the end, his spirit and determination took him into the French open finals and made him a world-class winner.

Jose Higueras, one of Michael's coaches at the time, said, "I've been in tennis for years, and this is truly the most incredible match I've ever seen. Michael has the head of a champion."

After the awesome win against Lendl, Michael rose slowly above the other competitors to the last stage of battle.

Left, Michael was overcome by emotion after defeating world champion Ivan Lendl at the French Open in 1989; above, Ivan Lendl

Two weeks of exhausting clay court play finally paid off for the young tennis star. With his taking of the French Open championship, he became the youngest man ever, to win a "Grand Slam" event. He was also the first American to win the French Open in thirty-four years.

The making of this young champion began with the early encouragement of his parents, Joe and Betty Chang. Joe and Betty had met on a blind date in New York City. They had much in common. Their families were both from Mainland China. They were both studying chemistry. Soon they were married, and their first son, Carl, was born in 1969.

Michael Te Pei Chang was born on February 22, 1972. The Chang family was living then in Hoboken, New

Below left, Michael at three months; right, Michael at 1 1/2 with big brother Carl, 4, and dad Joe

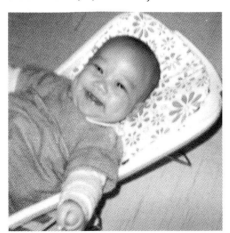

*Michael with his mom,
Betty, on his 9th birthday*

Jersey, but a change was in the air. When
Michael was two years old, the family
moved to St. Paul, Minnesota.

As Michael grew up, he and Carl
found lots of fun in their neighborhood.
Many children of all ages lived on their
street. This turned out to be a large and
friendly group. In the winter the
neighborhood kids bombarded each
other in furious snowball fights. When
the weather became warm, they
organized garage sales and outings to
"Secret Pond."

Secret Pond was the place where Michael first learned to love water creatures. He and his friends spent hours every spring catching tadpoles. As the tadpoles grew, their tails shortened and disappeared. Legs sprung out on the sides of their round bodies. Soon they turned into tiny frogs. A catch of this kind was definitely respectable. But sometimes they were able to catch a large, full-grown frog. That was really something to brag about!

By 11, Michael was already an expert fisherman.

Michael (middle row, fifth from right) smiles for the camera with his fifth grade class in San Diego.

There was another special thing about spring: tennis. From the time he was a little boy, Michael had been watching his dad play tennis. Joe played in small tournaments at the park near their home. The year Michael turned six, his mom suggested he try the game too. So he did.

Joe turned out to be an important coach for Michael and Carl. He tirelessly taught them to perfect their game. He set up matches. He gave Michael the first pointers that led to his desire to compete and win.

Michael was eight years old the first and only time he ever broke a tennis racket. He and his dad had been playing a game together. When Joe won the match, Michael was very disappointed! The desire to win was

Michael got his first tennis tips from watching his dad play.

Above left, Michael was San Diego's Boys 10 Champion at age 8; right, Michael (with brother Carl) made a big catch at La Costa Creek in California.

stronger than ever now. Michael began entering competitions and doing well.

Michael was always thinking about what he wanted to do when he grew up. With his parents both being chemists, he had a natural interest in science. Sometimes he thought he might like to be a doctor — a pediatrician or a veterinarian. He had learned to love fishing, too. He felt he could be a good fisherman or an oceanographer.

But tennis was becoming more and more important to him. Joe and Betty saw that their sons might excel at the sport. So when Joe was offered a job in San Diego, California, the family moved west. The warmer, sunnier climate of southern California was also perfect for outdoor sports.

Michael's mother would say, "We have a saying in Chinese, *Mung mu san tien.* It means a mother will move many times just for the sake of the child."

The move to San Diego meant many changes. There was not a big group of neighborhood kids to play with. But the Pacific Ocean was nearby. There was also Box Canyon, where Michael could go bass fishing and hiking. Best of all, in San Diego Michael could play tennis all year long.

Michael was a boy who loved challenges. He became involved in many sports. He especially liked soccer and basketball. But tennis and fishing were his favorites. Fishing gave him a sense of calm, strength, and peace that he carried into his other activities, especially tennis.

Michael was allowed to play tennis four times a week, but only if his homework was finished. His parents

Michael has always been dedicated to tennis practice.

had been raised to believe education was very important. They had studied hard to achieve their goals. They felt their sons should do the same. Michael did well at school and also on the tennis court. He was determined to excel.

"It's genetics," he believes. "I'm very competitive, like my parents. I never want to be second best, whether in school or in sports. I thrive on competition."

Michael was soon a strong player in junior tennis. In 1984 and 1985, when he was twelve and thirteen, he won important junior events. He began to notice that some talented tennis players never did their best because they didn't work at it. He saw that there were no short cuts to the successes he desired. Understanding this, he worked even harder.

A big step came in 1987, the year Michael turned fifteen. He was short and very thin, but he had more determination than some boys twice his size. That year, he became the youngest player at the time ever to win the prestigious U.S. Junior Championships. That tournament gave him the opportunity to compete at the U.S. Open.

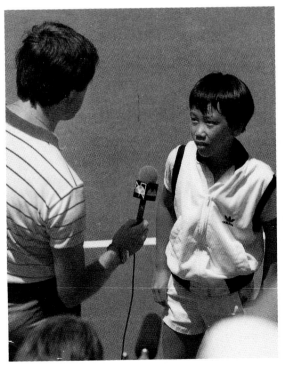

Left, Michael was interviewed by the press after winning his first National title, at 12 years old; below, Michael, again at 12, posing with actor Dick Van Patten in 1984.

Michael, 14, and Carl, 17, won the First International Boys 18 Doubles title at Taipei, Taiwan, in 1986.

Michael reached the second round of that event, making him the youngest player ever to win a match in that tournament.

By 1988, Michael had reached a turning point. He had gone as far as he could go in the juniors. He needed greater challenges to improve his tennis skills. The next step was turning professional. Becoming a professional tennis player meant Michael would have to leave high school. But he was only sixteen. This was a big decision for a boy whose family valued education so highly.

Michael and his family discussed the matter. If he left high school, he would only be able to graduate if he studied on his own. At the same time, he

Michael and Carl with friends at San Diego High School, where they both attended.

would have to train and compete professionally. It was a difficult decision. Finally, Michael chose to join the pros. At sixteen, Michael passed the final exam that allowed him to receive his high school diploma.

In the pros, the pressure was really on. The well-known professional tennis players had their eyes on Michael. Everyone wanted to see exactly what he was made of.

Michael quickly displayed poise under pressure. He performed well in many matches. He began to travel to major tournaments all over the world. Betty left her job as a chemist to travel with him as often as possible. She offered much support and encouragement, trying to make his life on the road as normal as possible.

"We've tried to take the best of Western culture and the best of Eastern

culture and make it into our culture,"
she would say.

The next year Michael showed just
how much his tennis playing had
matured. He set another record in early
1989. He became the youngest ever to
rank in the top twenty tennis players
worldwide. At the same time he was
gearing up for the big one — the 1989
French Open in Paris.

Michael's wall of trophies at home in Placentia, California

Michael experienced some extremely tough matches in that tournament but continued to win. He dramatically outwitted world champion Lendl. Then, in the finals, he beat Stefan Edberg and took the French Open trophy. The year before he had finished number 30 among the pros. With his French Open win, he shot to the number five player in the world.

above left, Michael exerts himself against Ivan Lendl at the 1989 French Open; right, Stefan Edberg, whom Michael beat to take the championship at the French Open.

This made him the youngest person ever to reach the top five. "These two weeks are going to stay with me the rest of my life," he said later.

The rest of 1989 was hectic but not as dramatic for the young tennis champ. He performed well at Wimbledon in England and in the U.S. Open. But in December he had a stroke of bad luck.

While practicing, he fractured his hip. The injury put Michael out of competition for a long time. He couldn't even pick up a tennis racket for two months. It took him until April 1990 to start playing regularly again.

The injury caused Michael much discouragement in the beginning. He understood that the risk of injury was always a possibility in sports. Yet, 1989 had been a year of incredible highs and lows. He realized that he needed time to reflect on the changes in his life. "In a way, it was kind of a blessing," he says now. A deeply spiritual person, Michael spent time studying the Bible while his hip was healing.

"I put so much pressure on myself I couldn't perform," Michael admits. "I want to be the best person I can be, because people are out there watching. I want to be able to touch their lives in an encouraging way." He feels his devotion to God helps him accomplish this.

After fracturing his hip, Michael trained with great determination to get back in shape.

Michael and his family in China

In all of his travels, Michael meets with many young people. He has inspired kids in countries all over the world. He's met with young people from rural areas as well as with inner city children in large cities such as San Francisco and Washington, D.C. He has even traveled to China, his parents' homeland, to play in exhibition tennis matches and to give clinics.

"The people of China are very warm and loving," Michael said after his visit there. "They are very curious. They want to know more about life outside their country."

Michael also wants to know more about everything. Besides the many tennis matches he plays each year, Michael also acts as a spokesperson and consultant for several companies. Because he is a busy, well-known athlete, Michael is advised by a

Michael caught in a tense moment during a match against Jimmy Arias at the U.S. Open in 1990.

Michael shakes hands with Jimmy Connors, another tennis great, after beating him in a match at the 1991 French Open.

worldwide management company, Advantage International. This company assists Michael and his family in their business dealings.

Michael's brother Carl is also an excellent tennis player. Since Carl graduated from college in 1991, he has been able to travel with Michael to tennis tournaments all over the world. As Michael's coach, Carl helps him

Michael after defeating John McEnroe during the 1991 U.S. Open

improve his game. "I do get upset in practice when I can't accomplish a certain thing," Michael admits. But he is an extremely strong player and has remained in the top ranks of professional tennis. His agility and remarkable court speed have earned him the reputation as one of the fastest players in the game.

Michael is a determined young man who has given up a "normal" life to do his best in the sport he loves. There are times when he would like to live like other people his age, but he accepts that his life is different. "For any career you pursue," he says, "if you want to be the best, you have to make sacrifices."

Michael's sacrifices have led to many tennis prizes and worldwide fame. He has set the record as "youngest ever" in numerous events. Still, one of his proudest moments came not from tennis but from fishing. He hooked an eight-pound carp after a tennis tournament in Cincinnati, Ohio.

Michael clenches his fist after winning in straight sets against Petr Korda in 1991.

"Fishing is more difficult than tennis in a way," the young champion claims. "It is much more complex and more preparation is needed."

Michael believes that his tennis technique can always be made better. He believes it is the same with life in general. "You can always improve," he says. "There are still many things I haven't learned."

Michael backhands the ball to an opponent during Britain's Wimbledon Championship in 1989.

Another great win for Michael, this time in Paris.

Someone may occasionally catch Michael in a serene moment on a lake, fishing pole in hand, away from the bright lights and the big crowds. But usually he will be found relentlessly training; constantly traveling to tournaments; always aiming for the highest and the best he can be in his chosen sport. His is not an ordinary life. But that is this young man's sacrifice, one he gladly makes.

MICHAEL CHANG

1972 Born February 22 in Hoboken, New Jersey, the second of two sons

1974 Moves to St. Paul, Minnesota

1980 Began entering tournaments in San Diego, California, where the family was now living

1984 Won the U.S. Tennis Association *Junior Hardcourt Singles*

1985 Won the *Fiesta Bowl 16s*

1987 Youngest player to that date (15 years, 6 months) to win the *U.S. Junior Championships*, giving him the chance to compete at the *U.S. Open*

Reached second round at the *U.S. Open*, making him the youngest player ever to win a match in that tournament

1988 Turned pro in February

Won first pro title in September in San Francisco

Played on *U.S. Davis Cup* team and won both singles matches against Paraguay

1989 In May, became youngest player (17 years, 2 months) ever to rank in the top 20 best

In June, became youngest ever (17 years, 3 months) *French Open/Grand Slam* champion; first American male to win French Open since 1955

In August, became youngest player (17 years, 5 months) ever to rank in the top 5

Champion, *Transamerica Open*, San Francisco, California

Champion, *Silk Cut Championship*, Wembley, England

1990 Champion, *Players International Canadian Open*, Toronto, Canada

1991 Champion, *Diet Pepsi Indoor Challenge*, Birmingham, England

1992 Champion, *Volvo Tennis/San Francisco*, San Francisco, California

Champion, *Newsweek Champions Cup*, Indian Wells, California

Champion, *Lipton International Players Championships*, Key Biscayne, Florida

Joined the U.S. Olympic tennis team in Barcelona, Spain

INDEX

ABOUT THE AUTHOR

Pamela Dell was born in Idaho, grew up in Chicago, and now lives in Los Angeles. After deciding at the age of five that she should be a writer, she began to write stories and published her own magazine, with a friend, at the age of eleven. Besides writing for children, she has published short fiction for both adult and young adult readers. She has also worked as a writer and editor in the fields of computer software, advertising, and entertainment, as well as many others.